November and Everything After

Egoboy Studios
Sunland CA

ISBN-13: 978-0615481258

ISBN-10: 0615481256

$12.50

Book One:

The Final Days
of Rock and Roll

by
Damien Stednitz

An Egoboy Studios Production

This book is dedicated to Patrick Jungers and Aaron Salmi. Without their generous support this book would have never happened. They are Carter and Harper's godfathers, my constant concert wingmen, and two guys I am lucky to call friends in these final days of rock and roll.

Author's Note

First off, I would like to thank my incredibly talented sister Tessie for going all-in with me on this crazy project. I continue to be humbled by your talents and am really proud that we were able to pull this thing off.

Next, I need to thank my wife Jayme who gave birth to our beautiful daughter while Tessie and I were working on this project. Thanks babe you are the best proof-reader, cheerleader, friend, editor, etc. etc. a boy could ask for.

Also my son Carter is in need of thanks for his willingness to appear in promotional materials and on the cover of the book.

I need to thank Eric and Jeff Holder for supplying the Kickstarter trailer with music. Please check out their band Redlo because they are fantastic. Also Eric's wife Melanie took the title page photos for me so thanks go out to the whole Holder clan.

Lastly, I need to give tremendous heartfelt thanks to everyone who supported this project on Kickstarter. I don't know what to say other than thank you for supporting Tessie, me, and art in general.

The following individuals deserve special recognition for going above and beyond in their support of this project:

Aaron Salmi
Pat Jungers
Connor Stednitz
Doug & Jean Chadwick
Mary Shirley
Jamie Reimer
Sony & Ken Coshow
Paula Lavigne
Jessica Kolterman
Joe Goetz
Terry McCarty
Dave Whitt
Tammy Blevins-Gierson
Alex Meyer
Lorraine DuRocher
Jason Grundmann
Ryan Johnston

Setlist

Soundcheck

The Final Days of Rock and Roll

I will be able to tell my son's sons that I was there at the end
The last waning days of rock and roll
I was the stegosaurus staring at the comet in the sky
Knowing it was important, but not really understanding
What it was or what it meant

It's a Wednesday night, I'm wearing a beanie
To hide the fact that I've shaved my head
To hide the fact that I'm going bald
There's two college girls that I don't know
Dressed in black that I'm pressed up against
Not because I'm into them, but because there's
Two bikers behind me pressed up against me
Not because they're into me, but because there's
Another 800 guys and 12 other girls pressing
Up against them, in a tiny club
In a neighborhood none of us go to
Except when we go to this club

In front of the college girls
Is the barricade, beyond the barricade
Is the curtain
Behind the curtain
Is The Rock and Roll

Lights go down, scream, scream, scream
Curtain drops
(rock curtains never open, they drop)
Mike Ness comes out
(if you're down, you know who he is, if you're not down
just know Mike Ness = cool rock star, 50 years old)
Mike has an acoustic guitar
He plays Johnny Cash

College girl to my right tells college girl who's stepping
On my toe, "Oh my God, it's that song from the Reese
Witherspoon movie"
I try to mentally teleport them into a ring of fire with no luck
(this is my first glimpse of the pending comet)

Acoustic guitar gets handed to roadie
An electric guitar with actual strings, not buttons
That is plugged into an amp, not a PS3
Comes out

The strings vibrate across sensors which creates
An electrical response
That travels through the cord to the amp where the amp
Washes us in The Rock and Roll

The Rock enters my ears and bends all the fine hairs in my
Inner ear, some of them permanently, increasing the ringing
I always hear
My bones shake from the bass, vertebrae in my back pop
As 850 people in the small club all try to occupy
The same 3 feet in front of the stage that I occupy

I scream, happy
I'm drenched in sweat
I'm not on a treadmill like a hamster

The crowd pushes hard to the left
I scream, happy

We're swayed violently to the right
I scream, happy

One college girl is lost to the throng
Behind me the pit jumps, I watch a biker fall
Two junior high kids pick him up, a body surfer
Kicks me in the head
I scream, happy

The Rock hits us loud
Right between the eyes
Mike Ness jumps
The mob jumps
I hit the barricade
My sternum bruises
The Rock hits us loud
I scream, happy

Some guy I don't know
Gives me a fist pound and a beer
The Rock hits us loud
I scream, happy

I thrash to stay above water
The water, a sea of bodies flooded
In sound, flooded in The Rock

There's no talking
Only Rock
There's no texting
Only Rock
There's no market share
Only Rock
There's no mortgage
Only Rock
There's no CNN
Only Rock
There's no me, there's no you
There's only the sea of us

And the music
And the music hits us loud

The song stops
And we scream, happy
I scream, happy
In these final days of rock and roll

First Set

Carter Beats the Devil, Damien Beats the Terminator

June, 2010 – Burbank, CA

Chuck E. Cheese is heaven or hell depending on your age. I walk in with Carter and the combined smell of toddler-mob, cheap pizza and cotton candy make me a little queasy. Carter's eyes bounce from screen to screen as the collective beeps and whistles from forty of the early nineties' finest arcade and carnival-style games send him into an ADD fit. I'm convinced that the guys that make Strattera have a silent partnership with Chuck E. Cheese.

The girl at the velvet rope stamps mine and Carter's wrists linking us together with a secret UV code so no randoms can walk out with Carter. Security measures completed, I feed a twenty into the token machine and we're off into the heart of Toddler Vegas.

We start at skee ball. Carter in his three years has developed an affinity for the game and a remarkable technique. He's one of the few overhand throw skee ball players I've met. He can also play skee ball for forty minutes on one token because his overhand throws bounce off the protective screen covering the skee ball target and roll back to him.

We're about twenty minutes into Carter's throw-bounce-rollback euphoria when Chuck E. himself makes an appearance. I hate this rat. The kids, Carter included, bum rush Chuck. He pats their heads and gives them politically correct hugs where he hugs each kid as if they had a small force field around them. Carter gives Chuck E. a high five and I give Chuck a nod that communicates I don't like him.

To be clear, I have nothing against the probable 15-year-old in the rat suit making minimum wage. This kid is fine with the exception that his part-time job sucks. He should be smashing lemons at Hot Dog on a Stick or pretending he's a badass at Hot Topic. No, it's Chuck E. Cheese *the character* that I dislike. I don't like the idea, the philosophy that surrounds Chuck E. Cheese. This single-skateboarding-rat-DJ concept that these young kids love, it pisses me off.

I hate Chuck for the same reason I don't like Yoko Ono or Courtney Love: he broke up the band. The band in Chuck's case was The Rock-afire Explosion. See, Chuck E. Cheese *the establishment* used to be Showbiz Pizza. For any of you who grew up with an Atari you know what I'm talking about. Showbiz had this awesome robot animal band called The Rock-afire Explosion.

The Rock-afire Explosion had a gorilla in a bow tie that played piano, a robot spacedog on drums, a hillbilly bear on guitar, and a mouse cheerleader that I think sung. It was awesome. The first "concert" I ever saw in my life was The Rock-afire Explosion at Showbiz Pizza on my sixth birthday. They rocked my birthday. It was epic. Imagine your first concert and then add skee ball and pizza, awesome.

Chuck E. ruined all that. In the early nineties Showbiz got bought out by Chuck E. Cheese and the suits decided to have "concept unification." All Showbiz locations turned into Chuck E. Cheese while all of us 80's kids were busy being grunge rockers. The Rock-afire Explosion was scrapped and replaced by the rat. The rock band was replaced by a lone, skateboarding DJ. I'm still mad about it.

I explain all this to Carter after Chuck walks away. Carter ignores me and throws a skee ball that misses an Armenian girl's head by about three inches. She tells him he's playing it wrong as he wings another skee ball into the Plexiglas as hard as he can. I'm pretty sure he thinks the goal of the game is to make as loud of a smack as you possibly can. I tell him God loves to play skee ball, but he doesn't get the reference since it's not from *Wonder Pets* or *Backyardigans*. (It's a *Dogma* reference, try to keep up.)

I decide to "help" Cater with skee ball so the Plexiglas has a chance to see another day. I suck at skee ball because I always go for the super small 10K in the corner rather than just trying to get 4K or 5K every time. I prove to once again not be much help. After Carter gets his whopping 2 tickets from our underwhelming skee ball score of 4500 we move on. We play a nearly defunct rollercoaster ride where what has to be a VHS tape, judging by picture quality, plays a POV video of a rollercoaster while the chair vibrates, slightly. Carter's mind is blown. I almost laugh as I hear the rollercoaster tape start to rewind when the ride is done.

Carter is then off to his nirvana, his Mecca of any playland or amusement park: the tube deal thing. I anxiously run around the toddler-sized hamster-town trying to track which tunnel and/or tube Cater has meandered into. I'm horrified the Armenian girl that he almost killed during skee ball will extract some kind of malicious vengeance in a dark, unexposed corner of the tube. Carter comes out fifteen minutes later with no injury other than super static hair.

I'm stunned that I didn't have to subject myself to the humiliating adventure of climbing into the tubes after him which previous to this trip is always how tube town has ended. Something big has pulled him out of his cylindrical maze euphoria early.

"Spongebob!! Spongebob Car!!!" Carter yells as he dismounts from the tube.

His static-induced Einstein-hair is making him look a little nuts. My eyes scan where Carter is now running with his arms flailing in that hilarious, spastic way three-year-olds run to somehow keep balanced. The game is off to the side. *Nickelodeon Racers* is arguably one of the newer games on the floor. Atop the game is Spongebob in his car ready to race. I grab the tokens and chase down Carter. Underwater checkered flags await us.

December, 1991 – Gretna, NE

"Holy shit! Look...at...that."

Dustin is in awe.

My face is still thawing from the Hoth-like conditions outside. I have no interest in looking up at anything other than the steam coming off of my hot chocolate. Then I hear Arnold Schwarzenegger say a couple of key taglines and I look up. Next to the claw game sits a brand new *Terminator 2* arcade game. Schwarzenegger sits atop a Harley. The screen is double wide. Pointed at the screen are two of the sweetest looking plastic machine guns I've ever laid my fourteen-year-old eyes on. To say it's sexy would be the understatement of the decade. Dustin runs to the player 2 gun.

"Pump-action grenade launchers!"

Pump. Action. Grenade. Launchers. Christmas has come a couple days early this year here at the Flying J truck stop. We're about to blow some shit up.

June, 2010 – Burbank, CA

We're a lap away from finishing 2nd and losing unless somebody does something about this fucking starfish. *Nickelodeon Racers* is a total *Mariokart* rip-off, but you know what? *Passenger 57* ripped off *Die Hard*, doesn't mean it's not a sweet movie. Anyways, we have a starfish problem.

Carter sits on my lap with his hands resting on the steering wheel. I handle all shifting, gas, brake and probably 85% of the steering. As we collect items a red item button flashes. When Carter hits it we throw the item to make other racers crash (again, just like *Mariokart*). Carter lives to hit the flashing button. Making other racers crash by throwing bubble bombs, trashcan lids or fish at them is to Carter what an acoustic set by Pearl Jam in my living room would be to me.

We rev up behind the starfish. We've got about a fourth of a lap left. It's now or never. Carter punches the button before I even need to tell him to. A trashcan lid appears in Spongebob's hand that he immediately wings into the starfish's head.

"Tartar Sauce!" the starfish yells (it's the voice of the guy that played Dauber on *Coach* btw) and we zoom past him to the finish line. Carter squeals and immediately begins asking for more. I'm pretty Chucked out so I let the "continue?" countdown to zero. We are about to leave when the high scores list pops up.

"What the hell?" I say which Carter immediately repeats. I award myself five points for not going with my standard, "What the fuck?"

The reason for mine and Carter's perplexity is there atop the high score list, with over 3 million points, sits the name: SATAN.

December, 1991 – Gretna, NE

Dustin and I are entranced as the game cycles through its various preview screens. The game includes actual clips from the movie. Let me repeat, there are actual clips from the movie interplayed into the game. Our minds can barely wrap around this concept. Guns N' Roses' *You Could Be Mine* plays from the game as Schwarzenegger shoots Robert Patrick in the head with a 10 gauge shotgun. I burn my throat because I'm now gulping my hot chocolate. Dustin throws off his gloves like a hockey forward ready to throw down.

"We have got to play this," he says. His eleven-year-old mind deciding that this is a worthy goal in life.

I nod silently in agreement.

"What are you guys doing?" my Dad asks, "Oh wow *Terminator 2*, cool."

Dustin and I don't hear the last part though, both of us are focused on the bucket he has under his arm. The bucket has all that we want. The reason we're at the Flying J at 5:30 in the morning on the first Monday of Christmas break is my dad is loading the newspaper machine with this morning's paper. My family is the local distributor.

Monday is key because it's when you empty the box of all the money from Sunday. Sunday being the big $1.25 issue. The paper machine only opens on Sunday if you put in 5 quarters. We run through roughly seventy papers on a Sunday. These quarters now reside in my dad's bucket. A bucket holding over eighty dollars in it, eighty dollars in quarters.

June, 2010 – Burbank, CA

I am feeding a second twenty into the token machine while the Mexican guy behind me sighs an annoyed sigh. Carter is getting excited. He's not really sure what's happening, but he knows that two cups of tokens is a really good sign. Dumb things piss me off. Like Chuck E. Cheese, a fictional character, causing the demise of a fictional band. Dumb things like some knucklehead teenager thinking it's funny to put the name SATAN in after getting the all-time high score on a game made for little kids.

"More Spongebob?" Carter asks, eyes bright.

"Yeah buddy, more Spongebob. We're taking it down."

The Tarantino movie in my head has Carter and I walking over to *Nickelodeon Racers* in slow motion while The Chemical Brothers' *Block Rocking Beats* plays in the background. In my mind Carter and I flick cigarettes to the ground and pull off our Ray-Bans slowly as we sit down and turn the ignition. We are going to race to beat the devil.

December, 1991 – Gretna, NE

Dustin and I are eight dollars in and kicking ass. We're currently in the wasteland post-Skynet future. Dustin is uncannily good with his grenade launcher as he takes out a hovering spaceship that was threatening to take me out. I'm mowing down robotic exoskeletons at every turn. My hand mashes the reload button. We're going to take back the future.

June, 2010 – Burbank, CA

The squirrel in the spacesuit has just slammed me into the wall. Carter and I almost fall out of our seat as we spin the wheel rapidly trying to get back on the track.

"Son of a bitch!" I yell as we stop the spin. Carter repeats my cry and I make a mental note that my Dad of the Year plaque may have to wait another month. Carter hits the flashing button and the squirrel is encased in a wall of bubbles. We zip by.

"Dagnabit!" she exclaims. Dumbass squirrel.

December, 1991 – Gretna, NE

"Can you guys really beat it?" my dad asks.

"Yes!!!" Dustin and I exclaim in unison. There's only 8 seconds left before the "continue?" expires. The fate of the future hinges on our dad's decision.

"Alright, go get it," Dad says handing over the bucket to us. We now have carte blanche and the coolest dad in this or any possible futures.

June, 2010 – Burbank, CA

The levels are getting progressively harder. A little green guy that looks like a bean pushes us to 2nd place. I give a red head kid $25 and ask him to bring me back $20 in tokens. He has an honest face. He comes back with a cup that feels about right. Carter now gives me a high five after each race and yells, "Boo Ya!"

We have small group of three other kids watching us now. I'm not sure if it's because we're taking on such a noble endeavor or they're just waiting to play the game. If it's the latter, it's going to be a while.

December, 1991 – Gretna, NE

"On your left!"

"Shoot! Shoot! Shoot!"

"I'm out of grenades, pop that fucker!!!"

"On your right!"

"Shoot! Shoot!"

June, 2010 – Burbank, CA

We break a million five. After his "boo ya" Carter now has taken to jumping down and doing a little dance before climbing up for the next race. The dancing is starting to draw more of a crowd. The single moms are starting to whisper with interest. A dad with no wife present who is just throwing money wantonly into the a video game has potential. From their point-of-view I'm rich, a good dad or both. They don't get what Carter and I are really trying to do here.

December, 1991 – Gretna, NE

Dad's manning my gun while I get Mountain Dews for the three of us. I hear Dustin frantically yelling "grenade" over and over.

June, 2010 – Burbank, CA

Spongebob has just raced past 2 million. I'm climbing out and dancing with Carter now between each race. We're high-fiving random Mexican and Armenian kids. Chuck E. Cheese himself is watching us now. Some parents are clapping. It's getting weird.

December, 1991 – Gretna, NE

"Holy shit," Dustin says, "final level."

"Yep," I reply. I'm sweating. The bucket is quite a bit lighter. The crushed Mountain Dews are littered around us. Robert Patrick runs in front of a liquid nitrogen truck. Dustin and I find our groove. I shoot holes in the truck, spilling the nitrogen. Dustin shoots Patrick keeping him busy so I can continue to pool the nitrogen.

After ten minutes and the bulk of our remaining bucket quarters Patrick is frozen solid.

"Take it Dust!" I say with gravity.

"Hasta la vista, bitch!" With a pump of a grenade Dustin saves the future.

June 2010 – Burbank, CA

Carter can't do the math, but he can sense the importance. This is the final race. It's the race that puts us ahead of SATAN. We get off to an early lead. Carter knocks out the starfish and the squirrel early with fish torpedoes. I smash the bean-looking guy into the wall. We're in the lead when at the final lap a new item we haven't seen before hits us...a backpack.

"Vamanos!!!" the bitch says as she shoots past us.

"Dora, Dad!" Carter yells.

"I know buddy, I know." Shit. Dora the fucking explorer.

December 1991 – Gretna, NE

The ride home is full of accomplishment, but not quarters. I will not remember fifteen years later what I got for that Christmas, but I will remember that morning. My dad supplying us with quarters and letting boys be boys. I will remember Dustin lobbing the perfect grenade shattering Robert Patrick's T1000 and solidifying a perfect memory.

June 2010 – Burbank, CA

This bitch is getting on my nerves. We've got half a lap to take her and the bean guy down. I'm running low on patience and tokens. In my mind our adversary is no longer some dumb high school kid being a smartass. It's actually Satan himself and he just dispatched this bilingual adventurer to take us down. The crowd is worried. Chuck pantomimes that we're in trouble. I make a mental note to punch him in the balls as soon as the race is over.

I hit an item box. We've got the trashcan lid. I down shift. Carter and I skid over a ramp and hit a boost. We launch. I see Dora rounding the turn from the air. We land nearly on the bean guy. I pull hard to the right smashing him into the wall. The item button flashes. Dora is directly in front of us. Carter is one button push away from victory.

"You're clear kid! Now let's blow this thing so we can go home!"

Carter hits the button and the trash can lid sails hitting Ms. Explorer in the cabesa just before she crosses the finish line. Carter and I cross earning the bonus that propels us to the top of the leader board. Carter and I put in his name ahead of SATAN and then dance. Carter does a somersault and the Armenian girl gives him a hug. I know what they say about long-term memory not kicking in until about four or five, but I hope Carter remembers this; this moment with me where we beat the devil.

Clawing

McCormick is stoned and trying to win a blue puppy. He's playing the claw game at the bar. I let out a long sigh. I'm outside the bar watching him through the window. This is going to be a long night. I text Emily that I've found him. She'll be relieved. I walk in. Toni the bartender gives me a polite nod and points over to where Mick stands joystick in hand. I've been looking for my friend for the last four hours and it looks like he's been here the whole time playing with stuffed animals.

"Kevin coming in next?" Toni asks, "You all calling in sick from work tomorrow? I pegged you guys as more of the weekend crowd."

"Just grabbing Mick," I tell her with a wave of the hand letting her know to leave it be.

McCormick doesn't acknowledge me as I approach. He's focused on the cheap, chrome claw dropping into the sea of plush. The inept claw caresses the blue puppy, grabs at it weak as an invalid and then retracts upwards empty. McCormick puts in another 5 dollars without reaction.

"Hey man, we gonna call it a night?" I say putting my arm on his shoulder. He looks like absolute shit. I can smell the stale weed on him. His eyes look hollow. I'm missing something here. He's off...this is something I haven't seen from him before.

"Em call you?" he asks quietly still staring ahead as the claw lands once again on the puppy only to again come up empty. The puppy is packed in tight between a tiny Oklahoma State basketball and a plush race car with the word "ninja" on it. There's no way the dog is coming out tonight.

"Yeah, she called. She doesn't know where you are and she's freaked. You guys get into a fight or something? She said you're not answering your phone."

Mick is the one person on earth who loves Emily Flowers more than me. A million years ago Em and I were an item for three awkward weekends. We mutually agreed that we were better friends than we were a couple. We met James "Mick" McCormick later our sophomore year. He was the smartass voice of hilarity in an otherwise painful Spanish class.

Emily jokes that we both started dating him around the same time. Em and Mick were and are a much better couple than Em and I were. When they were getting married Mick and I had to convince Em that I couldn't be the best man *and* the maid of honor. These people are family to me.

Emily called me tonight upset. Mick hadn't come home from work and hadn't called. After a few hours she got worried and called to see if he was with me. He wasn't. It was weird. Mick's not the type to just not show up. I asked her if they had had a fight or anything and she said no. I called around. I finally called Toni at the bar on a long shot. So now here we are: Mick ignoring me as he puts another 5 into a claw machine game at a dive bar where some weekends we play darts and watch college football.

"Mick, what the hell is going on man?" I lean my face into his field of vision blocking his view as the claw drops.

Mick pauses. He looks through me and without taking his hand off the joystick he destroys the world.

"Kaylie has cancer, Wayne."

I hear the claw land with a muffled thud or maybe it's my heart dropping. Kaylie is five. She has pig tails and her parents are two of the people that I care the most about in the world. I've known her since she was about an hour old. We saw *Tangled* together recently. She calls me "uncle."

"She has cancer, Wayne. Not me, not Emily. Kaylie. Kaylie has cancer." McCormick is dead behind the eyes, hollow. The claw retracts. It returns to its resting position. There are no words.

"Mick, I'm sorry, I...how?" The bar is gone. It evaporates. The world is my friend and a claw game. My face is wet. Somewhere far away I hear a five dollar bill go into a bill changer. There's a subway in my ears. Mick stares ahead at the game his knuckles white on the controller. His thumb jams the button. The claw drops, lazy, nowhere near the intended puppy.

"A few weeks ago, we took her in because her legs were hurting. You remember? We didn't come over that Sunday."

"Yeah, I thought that was the flu or something." My mind reels. I run through interactions. Had I missed any warning signs? Missed any chances to do more sooner?

"That's what we thought. Doc took some blood. He called me at work and said her white blood count was through the roof. He wanted to send it to a specialist. I didn't tell Em because I didn't want her to worry if it ended up not being anything. Guy called me today and said it's cancer, no question."

The claw errantly grabs a teddy bear and drops it right at the edge of the opening.

"I thought K was feeling better. Emily said she was doing better this week." I hear my mouth say.

The claw retracts and heads back to its start position.

"Yeah, she's not doing better Wayne. She has fucking cancer." The claw wobbles out again.

"Is she going to be okay? What are her odds?"

The claw drops, Mick spins letting go of the joystick, my friend is not himself. He's an animal backed into a corner, scared, out of options. He grabs my jacket roughly.

"I don't know her odds SHE'S NOT A PAIR OF FUCKING POCKET ACES WAYNE!!! SHE'S...She's my little girl."

The bar stops. The world stops. The air is gone from the room. The anger seeps away from Mick as quickly as it rose. He has nothing left. I watch his eyes dim. He turns back to the claw game and absently plays. After three failed attempts he presses his head against the glass.

"I don't know what we're going to do. They don't know Wayne. They just don't know. They want her to start treatment this Friday. It's going to be rough...and they just don't know."

"Look man let's get you home, we can talk to Em."

"No! Look, this puppy, Kaylie wants it. It's from that TV show she watches. I ran in here with her a couple of weeks ago to drop off the fantasy football registration. She saw the damn thing and kept asking for it. I told her we didn't have time and she threw a fit. She kept saying we did have time. I told her we were in a hurry. I need to get this for her Wayne and then we can go."

My friend and I take alternating turns in silence. The claw drops. The claw retracts. The blue dog remains firmly wedged. I don't know what to say or do. Nothing is fair or right with the world. Mick shakes the game to loosen the prize. We line up the claw perfectly. We drop it just right. It picks up the dog for a moment and then drops it. This happens over and over. In spite of our best efforts the claw can't hold on. It's late. We're out of time.

"Mick we should go and get you home."

"Yeah, I think we're going to take some time. Maybe take Kaylie to the coast before she has to start treatments. She likes the beach."

"That's good man. Do that."

"Yeah," Mick says, distant. I wonder if he is seeing the beach and his daughter running toward the ocean in his mind. Bare feet, sand, waves, laughter, and Kaylie running, effortlessly, to the horizon. His eyes close and he presses his forehead against the glass of the machine for what seems like days.

He then punches through the glass of the claw machine. Safety glass rains around us. Mick grabs the dog.

"She has time Wayne. I'm going to show her."

I watch my friend walk out into an indifferent, rushing world and an uncertain future. I stay to talk Toni down. I write a check to protect my friend. The claw hangs exposed unnecessary now. It remains ready unaware everything has now changed. It is unaware of its failure. It is blameless because sometimes you line up everything right, do everything right, and you still just can't hold on.

Second Set

Four Eighteen

In 4 minutes and 18 seconds you can do a lot.

You can
drink an entire Big Gulp.
You can
watch *Jedi* up to the part where Luke goes to Jabba's palace.
You can
burn up most of your time at an open mic.
You can
watch a little of CNN and then feel bad about the world.
You can
login to Facebook, status update, and then log back out.
You can
move exactly 8 inches on the 405.
You can
make three peanut butter and jelly sandwiches

or

you can
sing along to your favorite pop song turned up really, really
loud.

I'd do that.

All in All You're Just Another
Yellow Brick in the Road

So I decided to see about this whole
Pink Floyd / *Wizard of Oz* sync-up
thing last Friday.
I made sure I started *Dark Side of the Moon* right at
the 2nd MGM lion roar (apparently this is to ensure sync-up).
I got to the part in *Oz* where it all switches to color
but *Dark Side* hasn't gotten to *Any Colour You Like*
before I gave up.
It doesn't work.
I noticed no "sync-up" as the internet had promised
(except during the tornado scene which was kind of cool).

I was about to turn off the movie when Jayme came down
and freaked because *The Wizard of Oz* was on.
She got giddy and ran to make popcorn.
We sat on the couch and ate a bowl of buttered popcorn
and M&M's. The candies melting like the witch would.

I forgot how much I liked this movie.
I forgot how as a kid I would religiously watch it during
the annual showing on TNT.
I told Jayme I used to sing *If I Only Had a Brain* in school.

We laughed.
We agreed the flying monkeys were freaky little creatures.
We agreed Judy Garland was a beautiful little creature.
Our hands kept finding each other
beneath buttered, chocolate kernels.
After the movie I put Pink Floyd on again
on vinyl this time.
We lit some candles.

There was a bar in downtown LA that had two open seats last
Friday because I realized that, in the end,
Dorthy was right.

.com / passion

my phone is my camera
which is my calendar
which is my arcade game
which is my cd player
which is my typewriter
which is my price scanner
which is my email
which is my photo album
which is my Facebook
which is my social outlet
which is my interaction

I never go outside
my eyes to the screen
your eyes to the screen
you screen, I screen, we all screen

and screen
and screen
and screen

we talk with our thumb
until we're all dumb

and numb
and numb
and numb

I have the entire world
next to my car keys in my pocket but...

I had a dream last night
about a girl

she held my hand

Curbside Christmas Trees

It's January 10th in Pasadena
There's no snow but it's cold
I'm driving aimlessly down California
I haven't had anywhere to be

It's 16 days after Christmas in Pasadena
The Rose has come and gone
Colorado is littered with debris
I'm starting to really feel old

It's a grey 6 a.m. in Pasadena
On each curb lays a dead Christmas tree
The garbage truck lumbers on Marengo
Filled with Christmas crushed and bent

It's January 10th in Pasadena
There's no snow but it's cold
It's a grey 6 a.m. in Pasadena
On each curb lays a dead Christmas tree

They litter the rearview
I pull over to the curb and get out
I sit among the discarded
I close my eyes and wish for snow

This Smaller Murder

Kevin tells me that a group of crows is called a murder
Herd of cows, flock of seagulls, murder of crows
This is the kind of stuff that Kevin knows, random facts
Sputtered out like hot oil in a broken engine

Kevin and I shared a babysitter as children
I liked him then because he made me laugh
I still like him now
His thick glasses, constant smile, sporadic verbal gunfire
Kevin's simple delights in birds or ice cream or the wind

Three crows that live in the tree outside my bedroom window
Remind me often of Kevin
Make me call him on Saturdays when I don't want to
But when I know I should
On our calls he talks of crows (his favorite bird since *Dumbo*)
Or how the cornfields look when the wind hits them
Or his love of go-carts
Or how I am his friend
He reminds me of this often on our calls
I guarantee Kevin frequently that I will always be his friend

Kevin's mom dies unexpectedly, asleep at the wheel
She worked two jobs so Kevin could live at home
The family tree his mom and him occupied
Was a very small tree
Kevin and his mom were the sole branch

A county sheriff tells Kevin's nurse, she tells Kevin
She calls me
My crows sit on the branch outside the window
I talk to Kevin; try to calm him
This would be hard for anyone
It's impossible for him

Two weeks later I've already talked to social workers
Now I talk to Kevin and I explain to Kevin why he can't
Come live with me in Los Angeles
The crows stare at me intently
As I saw off Kevin's last branch
I guarantee him life in a cage
I assure him I'll call when he gets settled in at Oakdale

As the phone hits the cradle
My three crows take flight

I watch them fade into the sky

I am haunted by this smaller murder

I Am Not Mars, You Are Not Venus

you are Saturn
unique and beautiful
somewhat off center
a volatile surface with
unannounced raging storms
yet hypnotic
a standout among your peers

and I am Saturn's ring
shattered particles
frozen
forever circling
held by your gravity
unable to drift away

After Pat's Wedding

I wake up with a piece of cigar in my mouth
My cummerbund is around my head
I am in a tux, in a chair, in Nebraska
Groomsmen are littered around the room
Bed, floor, tub
Scott appears to be lying next to a girl that I'm pretty sure
Was the bartender
Aaron, a brother from college, appears to be wrapped in
What I'm assuming was the curtain

I get to wobbly feet, track down my two rented cuff links
In the bottom of a half empty glass of jungle juice
My plane back to LA leaves in three hours
I stand in the doorway
Staring at my former crew of college cohorts
The "Nebraska buddies" as my wife calls them
Memories of times past litter the room as much as tux pieces

Pat was the last of us to get married, the final reception
In the hallway, I tape a note of congratulations to the door of
The honeymoon suite and head to the elevator

The elevator doors close on my past
When they open again I have matured
I call my wife as I head through the lobby
I walk out of the hotel, the sunlight finds me
Hungover
Heading forward into my 30's
I never look back again

Angry Birds

there's other things I should be doing right now
I could be being a better

dad...husband...friend...employee...status-updater

I could be working out...flossing ...writing

I'm not
because I sold my soul for 99 cents
I'm not
because that green bastard with the helmet
is laughing at me
he's laughing this guttural chuckle
that echoes in my head like
Mark Fisher's laugh down the hallway
as I'm walking away in 2nd grade

all of a sudden I'm Robert Deniro
all of a sudden my index finger is Jason Statham
all of a sudden my feet are bloody, my tank top is filthy
and the hand gun is taped to my back with Christmas tape
my fury is red, yellow, blue, white and black
my fury is taut, pulled back, potential energy
ready to flare kinetic

empires crumble
friends are lost
worlds vanish

stone, glass, wood and flesh bleed
the 60's had LSD, we have LCD

heads slam into virtual walls

yippee-ki-yay

Spin

It's Monday.
I'm lying on a table shirtless while the nurse apologizes she doesn't have time to shave
me. She covers my chest in stickers that will be attached to electrodes. My head spins.
The taste of baby aspirin dries my mouth. I'm getting an EKG. I am having a heart attack.

It's Wednesday.
I'm standing in front of a room of salespeople, my salespeople. I'm in my power suit.
I'm explaining the plan to grow our market share even though the economy is imploding.
I spin it as a good thing for us. Heads nod. I'm getting good buy-in. I tell them we're all going to win.

It's Tuesday.
I push through the spinning doors at the hotel. I'm wearing a pull over with my company's logo on it. I see a group of my counterparts at the lobby bar. The meeting doesn't start until tomorrow. I grab a drink. There's still stickers from the EKG stuck to my chest. No one knows.

It's Monday.
I'm in bed when my heart begins to beat out of my chest. I can't breathe. Everything spins out of control. I wake up Jayme. In ten minutes I'll leave for the emergency room.

It's Wednesday.
My team is clapping and cheering. They're pumped up. They head out of the meeting room high-fiving and talking about the big quarter we're going to have. I stay back. The room spins. No one sees me shaking, hands against the table, catching my breath in gulps.

It's Monday.
It's 3am and the doctor is telling me I'm not having a heart attack.

It's Tuesday.
At the bar upper management calls me the "Master of Spin".
Sales are up in a down economy.
I'm going to go far. I'm handed a cigar.

It's Monday.
The doctor tells me I'm having panic attacks. I feel stupid...weak. He spins it that at least I'm not having a heart attack. He tells me that I need to slow down. I feel stupid...weak.

It's Wednesday.
I'm sleeping in a hotel bed. I've slept at home two nights this month, one of which I spent in the ER.

It's Thursday.
My hands are shaking. No one sees.
It's Tuesday.
Hands slap my back.
It's Monday.
My hands cover my face.
It's Wednesday.
My hands clap to a sales cheer.
It's last Monday.
I'm in a hotel.
It's last Tuesday.
I'm in a hotel.
It's last Wednesday.
I'm in a hotel.
It's last Thursday.
I'm in a hotel.

It's Friday.

The meeting is over. I'm stuck in traffic by Camp Pendleton when a huge helicopter flies over me. I think it might land on my car. It's a Black Hawk. They are just amazing machines. If you met me when I was eight I would have told you I was going to fly a helicopter like that one when I grew up. I would not have told you that I was going to be a middle manager, the "Master of Spin".

The Black Hawk touches down on a landing pad in a chaotic yet graceful dance of motion, metal, and sound. I hear another coming in. I look to my right and there they are. At least ten Black Hawks heading my way. It's got to be some sort of training exercise. I pull over on to the shoulder and turn my hazards on.

The car behind me immediately speeds up to gain the eight feet that I've opened for him. I get out of my car, take off my tie, and climb up on the roof to sit. I sit Indian style like my brother and I used to at the drive-in in Omaha.

Helicopter after helicopter land. Dust clouds billow. Blades spin and spin and spin and spin to an eventual stop.

The traffic eventually breaks. Cars begin to move from their crawl to resume their breakneck pace. I stay and sit watching the Black Hawks land, chaos into calm.

Jayme calls. I let her know I'll be home soon. She asks if I'm doing okay. I tell her yes and mean it. I reach under my shirt and peel the last stubborn sticker from my chest. I watch the last helicopter blades spin slower and slower and slower into a stillness.

Caveman Frappuccino

I was in Starbucks on Thursday
thinking about buying *Akeela and the Bee* on DVD
when the man behind me actually ordered
a coffee

you could hear the record scratch
and everyone who was having their morning
milkshake disguised as a Frappuccino stopped

I had just finished ordering my vente hot cocoa
non-fat dairy, light on the whip please
when the haggard man behind me slapped down a five
and asked for the strongest thing they had, black, a large

I nervously chewed my apple fritter as they filled
his vente glass

he took several swigs in big gulps, surely burning his tongue
his calloused hand not needing the cardboard
heat protector thing
I gave him a wide berth as he walked past me
his flannel shirt had a hint of cigar

as he walked out
two guys with too small Ed Hardy shirts walked in
their frosted tips matched perfectly, Seacrest would have
been proud
I'm sure they thought we were all staring at them

unaware that the last real man in Los Angeles had just
walked out
a ghost
a dinosaur
an anachronism

Contrails

I'm
9 years old
In an alfalfa field
My fingertips muddy
As I have just dug the earth
And buried a spool of kite string
I lie on my back and stare into the sky
As the kite hundreds of feet above darts
And cuts through the sky, the string tugging
The earth that it is anchored to, I smile
I lie against the moist earth, exhale
I am on the verge of adolescence
But today there is only blue sky
And anchored plastic
String and earth
Perfect
Planes cut contrails into the blue innocent sky
I lie silent
The alfalfa
Shields
Me from
The world
I hear
Nothing
But wind
My eyes
Follow the
Planes
And kite
I am
Calmness
I am
Simplicity

I am
29 years old
My fingertips muddy
They have just dug earth
She is gone, we bury her today
She lies on her back inside the box
My brother finally breaks down as years of
Memories play inside my head, I go to the alfalfa field
I am still there, 9 years old, lying in the green, watching
I lie next to myself, this boy, silent and we smile
Watching the kite tug and circle against
The impossible flawless blue, I could
Stay here forever in this moment of
Kite and sky, peace and innocence
The boy sits up and digs, he frees
The string, my kite gives into
The wind, I rise and he takes
My hand and we watch
The kite free now
Diminish to sky
Plastic, string
Sky then
Gone
Planes cut contrails into the December winter sky
I stand silent
My memories
Shield me
From loss
I hear nothing
But wind
My eyes follow
Her down
I pray
She knows
Calmness
Simplicity

Heroin

I'm straight up addicted to heroin
I mean full on hooked
I think about it a lot
Not all of the time
But probably weekly, especially if I'm driving
I
Love
Heroin

Not the drug but
The song about the drug
By The Velvet Underground
It's the only song not by The Doors
On *The Doors Motion Picture Soundtrack*

It's a great, great song
If I could tie my arm off with my headphone's cord
And somehow inject this song's awesomeness
Directly into my veins
I would

It's like 8 minutes long
I miss two or three other songs because of heroin
Not a lot of people use or have heard of heroin
I played it for some people I work with at a meeting
They hated heroin, they said it was boring and slow
They don't understand

Heroin gets me
Heroin has got me
8 minutes at a time
Since college
Where I played it on my Discman
While swaying with Jayme slow

In a dorm room
Blue hues of mood lighting
Provided by her navy dress
Draped over
My lone desk lamp
A perfect 8 minutes
With her, my heroin

Friends can come and go
Like a pop song

But her...
Heroin is forever
I'll take another 8 minute hit of perfect
With her

Forever

We Live in Words

we live in words
hanging on them all

we live in card houses
waiting for the fall

wind wind when
I can't sleep

water wash after
I'm in too deep

crash crash crash
to it all

these fragile days
destined to fall

Text (Used to Be a Noun)

Charles Dickens used to release his
novels in serialized chapbooks
little bundles of text that came out monthly
people would line up waiting for the next issue
an emotional event for many
men and women reading as they walked home
no internet to carry ahead the ending and spoil it

Truman Capote and Dylan Thomas used to
read to sold out auditoriums
people packed in for poetry and prose before the podium
Thomas and Capote were rock stars before rock stars
their words flowing down the aisles
over the rows of rapt fans who listened in the ringtone free
vacuum of silence only a pre-1991 concert hall could create

I've had 40 free text messages a month for the last year
I sent my first text message today, it took me an hour
I was taught home row keys not thumb typing

my 15-year-old sister can type with her thumbs
as fast as she can talk, maybe faster
my first text message was to her

I'm texting her *Great Expectations*
a paragraph a day
I figure since she stops everything to read every text
she may as well read something worthwhile

we'll be finished in July of 2017

I like to think Dickens would be amused
a little electronic serialized chapbook

my sister is currently not amused,
but maybe she'll see the message in the text

Twenty All the Way

do you remember the
Tuesday it was raining and
we skipped class and
stayed in my dorm room
and listened to *Electric Ladyland*
on vinyl and drank Swiss Miss with
the tiny marshmallows you like and
we sat under that ratty quilt
your grandmother gave you
and we watched the storm
roll through and punish
the good kids running to class their
books overhead an inadequate umbrella
and there was a Dave Matthews
poster on my wall and the one corner
always was falling and
you stood on my desk to
tape it back and the next day
I turned in French papers
with your footprints...

that Tuesday, that Tuesday
was twenty all the way

I turn thirty tomorrow so maybe
we can dig up some records
and call-in today
and just stay in our
small bedroom
sit in bed together
in old t-shirts drinking
hot chocolate this
last day of twenty

it has been a good run

Blue

Now that everyone has a Bluetooth
I no longer can tell with any degree of certainty
Who is crazy and who is not

Spades (for Andrew Owen)

with a few beers
clubs
hearts
diamonds
and spades
you can create America
anywhere
because it's so ready made

HHH

I'm drunk
and the pink one

I haven't eaten a single
marble yet
because I snapped my head
off and threw it at Jayme

I still press the lever though

Wisdom

"Shit"
My dentist says

This is not a good sign
My bottom wisdom tooth has just broke
Causing the metal dental device to stab
Into my gum
I know this because of the swear word
My dentist has just uttered
And the blood spurting out of my mouth
All *Raging Bull* style

I'm cool about it
Not because I'm some
Deniroesque tough guy but

Because of Novocain
I feel nothing and am pretty stoked about it

My dentist begins digging the last few pieces of
The tooth out, my gum is getting fucked up
I'm watching it all in the reflection on his blood
Spatter visor thing he wears
It's a car wreck hypnosis situation for me
He's desperately trying to dig out the root
I'm surprised he's not using a chainsaw
Given the lack of finesse he's showing

I'm lying there, calm as a corpse
Trying to remember who sang that song
Novocain for the Soul (A: eels)
Wondering how useful it would be to have
Novocain on hand if I was about to get into
A fistfight or was about to be tortured to
Reveal the location of the microfilm

We have the technology to stop feeling on
Demand, within seconds, this needs to be
More readily available

I could have given some to you
When she left, and you tried to play it cool
Like you didn't care, like there wasn't that
Ring in the pocket of your good intentions
Like you didn't know you let things go
Untreated for too long so they rotted
At the core even if outwardly it all looked good
You pretending it didn't hurt when she
Extracted herself from your life, breaking off
In a bloody mess, while you tried to pretend
There wasn't that piece that you can't dig out
Still left
In you
To rot
While she healed
And flourished
Because she exercised some wisdom
You decaying
Holding an invitation
That could have borne your name

Spring

Jayme and I are playing with a Slinky
an honest-to-God Slinky
the old school metal kind
not that neon plastic one
that was cool in 1991
I'm talking about the real deal
Slinky

we bought it three hours ago on a whim
for the last hour we've been trying
to get it to go all the way down the stairs
in one, uninterrupted, perfect run

the dog is going nuts
the cat lost interest about twenty minutes ago

Jayme asks me if I'm ready from upstairs
I yell back yes
and our 49th run begins
the Slinky looks determined
good momentum
we're going to make it
that unmistakable slinky sound
finds its rhythm
three steps to go
two
one
the Slinky stops at my feet
with a climatic quiver of accomplishment
Jayme lets out a cheer
I whoop for the first time in like forever

our iPad and PS3 walk out of our place together
grumbling about what bullshit this all is
angry that for a perfect 60 minutes it was 1979
in our townhouse and we were young again

The Last Magician

I was having a bad week.
The only highlight being a free sandwich coupon
I had won at work.

It was a Friday night that was feeling like about
ten Wednesdays rolled into one.

I took my free sandwich coupon to the sandwich shop hoping
to have at least one cool thing happen to me, namely a
sandwich I didn't have to pay for.

On the cool front things were not looking good. I had to buy
a drink and chips to get the sandwich for free. I was about to
bitch to the clerk when eight girls all around the age of
twelve walked into the shop squeaking and beeping like mall
cash registers. The eight of them all seemed to be named
Madison and had smartphones for hands.

I took a booth and tried to focus on my mostly free roast beef
sandwich.

That's when I noticed the magician.

Green suit
darting eyes
doctor's bag filled with
scarves
rings
foam rabbits
and
perhaps
swords
to
swallow.

He was old.
I mean like really old.
His temples looked as if they were made
of tissue paper.
His hair looked as though he had made the effort,
but had ultimately failed in taming it.
He looked like someone's forgotten great-grandfather.

His suit at one time had probably been one of the nicer ones
out of the Sears catalog.
It now showed the years as much as he did.
Perhaps too many years of hiding doves in the sleeves had
ultimately done the suit in.

Everything was threadbare.

However, in spite of all the erosion
his eyes were still young, almost mischievous.
His bow tie was still tight and straight.

He had a smile/smirk on his face,
the kind that comes from knowing
what no one else knows.
Smirking, he began to shuffle cards absentmindedly.

The deck of cards in his hand were one of those
classic, worn decks of cards.
The kind you keep for years because
they have history and you're the only one that knows
the jack of hearts has a slight nick out of the corner.

These cards were fluid in his hand.
His long fingers defied their age.
I watched, in mid-chew, as the

ace of spades

disappeared

and then

reappeared

and then was

gone

again.

He just sat there shuffling occasionally glancing at the room
making sure we were noticing the whole
card-vanish-shuffle-thing.

The cards danced in his hands like a lover while he seemed
disinterested.

Madison #4 asked him if he was a magician.
His face lit up like someone had flipped a switch.
Teeth that were impossibly white flashed a grin.

"You want to see a card trick my little lovely lady?"

I silently answered "yes" in my head.

He stood up and began to perform for the Madisons who
were pseudo-interested.

I was enthralled.

I tried to catch the trick,
eye the scam,
break the code,
but I still have no idea how the
king of hearts
that Madison #6 picked made it to the top of the deck.

I had watched her firmly place it in the middle of the deck
just moments before.

Perhaps the Madisons were in on it?

Perhaps they were all scam artists out to dupe losers in their
mid-thirties who are eating roast beef subs that they got for
mostly free.

It didn't seem likely.

Then again, the idea that this old man possessed the ability
to make the king of hearts transmutate from one card into
the other seemed unlikely as well so who knows?

The magician was just getting warmed up.

He introduced himself as Reginald the Great to which more
than a couple of Madisons rolled their eyes.

I watched him make foam rabbits multiply while being held
in closed hands.
I watched cards change suits and number with a tap of a
finger.

It felt good to wonder again.
It felt good not to even begin to know how.
It felt good to see magic at 9:24 p.m. in a sandwich shop.

Ultimately my need for nicotine trumped my desire to be mesmerized. I finished my sandwich and left right about the time rings were being interlocked and unlocked.

As I killed yet another Pall Mall (and to a smaller degree myself) I watched Reginald the Great through the window.

The Madisons were losing interest. With each ring he made pass through the next he lost another Madison to the ring of a text message. By his last trick the Madisons were at best indifferent; some giggled at his expense.

I couldn't hear his pitch at the end when he passed his hat around. He never stopped smiling, but the defeat was in his body language.

Two Madisons gave him a dollar and one gave him a coupon for a mostly free sandwich.

I smoked another one and watched him pack up his scarves and then eat his sandwich quietly. He ate with an economy of movement. He no longer made eye contact with any other patrons.

I meant to tell him I loved his show when he came out, but my girlfriend called.

We were discussing which show to watch on our DVR after she got off the late shift when Reginald left. He passed me silently and was around the corner before I thought to say anything.

It began to snow.

I hung up.

I never saw another magician again.

Losing Nemo (a manifesto in nine parts)

I

it all started with central air
the isolation, the slavery
it all started with a desire to be cool
my grandparents, when they were in their twenties
and the temperature was in the eighties,
would go out onto their front porch to get cool
Donna would make a pitcher of lemonade
enough to share

sharing was a likely event because the neighbors
were all out on their front porches trying to get cool
so glasses were shared; talk flourished in the shade
children played in yards that were treated like common areas
neighbors became a neighborhood

progress pushed us into our homes
we barricaded ourselves in Freon-filled rooms
so much cooler
lemonade was regulated into single serving juice boxes
just enough for one
stab your straw in
so much cooler

II

my uncle met my aunt at a stoplight
in the 1960's
the temperature was well into the 70's
it was hot so his windows were down
so were hers
eyes met
smiles
a quick red-lit discussion
she agreed to pull over into the bowling alley parking lot

I have five cousins because of two windows that were rolled
down welcoming

III

I'm not making any progress down the 101
San Luis Obispo is barely behind me
Los Angeles is ten thousand unmoving car lengths away
my windows are sealed
ac blasting

I look to the car next to me
a young couple, cute
him: sharp haircut, loosened tie, confident smile
chatting away into a Bluetooth headset
her: blonde, bright eyes, dimples
looking at me, but talking into a camera
that has a phone built-in

IV

My mom and dad are driving me and
my brother to Worlds of Fun
in a magical, far away land called Kansas City
I'm 7, my brother is 4
we've already been told the drive from
Omaha to KC will take 4 hours

I-80 stops being familiar and soon we enter the boring part
of the drive
it's flat, everything looks the same
to pass the time I retell *The Empire Strikes Back*
to Dustin inserting dinosaurs at parts where I think the
movie would have been better had there been dinosaurs
Dustin laughs hysterically as my imagination finds itself
unbridled through necessity

a half-hour later after a Stegosaurus eats Luke's hand and
Darth Vader rides off on a Tyrannosaurus Rex
Dustin and I begin asking if we're there yet

our mom looks back and tells us about her first trip to an
amusement park when she was little
she takes us through the tea cup ride and the tilt-a-whirl
adding that Uncle Dan threw up on the scrambler
Dustin and I both laugh at this
that Thanksgiving we make fun of Uncle Dan
for being a such a wuss

my mom paints a picture of an amusement park
to the point where we can taste the cotton candy
Dustin and I spend the next hour discussing which
one of us is going to eat the most

our dad chuckles to himself as
I assert I can eat ten turkey legs
only to be topped
by Dustin's claim of eleven

I remember this drive better than the park itself

V

I'm still on the 101
languishing

the couple is still two feet away from each other
talking
but relying on cellular towers to take their words
convert said words into zeros and ones and relay these words
from tower to tower until it reaches the two individuals
somewhere else in the country to whom they are talking to
rather than just making eye contact and talking with the
spouse next to them

they pull ahead and I see their two sons in the back seat
watching *Finding Nemo* on dual screens
attached to the back of the seat

the two brothers watch a father scour the ocean for his son
their dad three feet away sends a text message
still talking on his Bluetooth

VI

I don't know my neighbors
none of us use the front door
we leave our air conditioned houses
get into our air conditioned cars
open our garage doors automatically
drive to work

when we get home the garage door opens again
we don't even have to get out of our car
the garage door closes behind us
we walk back into our air conditioned home

the process repeats

the air is not the only thing that is conditioned

VII

my sister's generation spends recess in computer labs
on Facebook counting friends that they IM and email
and send pictures and messages to, but they never sit on
swings and talk about their thoughts and dreams

VIII

baby's watch *Baby Einstein* until their old enough
to find Nemo
they watch the video at home on a flat screen until it's time
to go through the garage into the sealed car
Nemo comes with though

it's really only about a two minute pause
until it's back on again

parents are remote controls that sometimes give McDonald's

IX

I'm not being nostalgic
I'm not being old-fashioned
I'm not being paranoid

I'm being cautionary

we've got so much technology
so many cords that plug-in
we've got so many kids that plug-in

there's a reason that outlet is called *the power*

we've got to cut the cord
we've got to take the power back
we've got to have a blackout
so we can see the light

there's a generation that can't talk if there's not a signal
there's a generation that can't interact without a screen
there's a generation that's being raised by a clownfish

we've got to hang up
look over at each other and talk

we've got to read a damn book made of paper

we've got to shut down and relish
in the wonders of a backyard
we've got to lose Nemo and find our own children

we've got to have a black out
so we can see the light

we've got to lose the power
so we can find each other

Heat Waves Suck / Heat Waves Are Awesome

Despair.
Our air conditioner is broke.
I'm dying on the vine.
I'm sitting at the kitchen table
fingers slowly moving across
my sweltering keyboard.
I'm working out of the home today;
a self-imposed sweat shop.
It's 9 a.m. and it's already 90 degrees outside.
I've eaten 3 of Carter's Otter Pops.
My tongue is purple and I'm still hot.
I want to die.

Jayme comes down the stairs, sweating.
She's wearing nothing but a drenched, clingy half tank-top
and a pair of Hello Kitty panties.
She grabs a bowl of cereal and sprawls in the papasan.
Her legs dangling just off the floor, she is all sweat, tan and
tattoos.
She is Miami.
She is South Padre.
She is New Orleans.

A jazz band plays in my head.

I am filled with hope,
love,
and other drugs.

Slow Dancing Stairway (w/ thanks to DF for showing me the way)

Stairway to Heaven
is the single greatest rock song
of all time

don't talk to me about *Free Bird,*
Yesterday, or *Comfortably Numb*
or anything recorded after 1980
I don't want to hear about it
(you'd be wrong anyways)

Stairway is it

Led Zeppelin IV was the 5th CD
I ever owned

the first four CD's being, in order:
Vivid and *Time's Up* both by Living Colour
He's the DJ, I'm the Rapper by DJ Jazzy Jeff
and the Will Smith
and *The Simpsons Sing the Blues*

Guns N' Roses, Nirvana and Pearl Jam all followed
but *Zep IV* set the stage
track 4, *Stairway to Heaven*, set the baseline
by which all future songs would be judged

when we first started dating
Jayme only listened to Journey
it was one of two cassettes she had
the other was The Police's *Greatest Hits*

I used to play the Journey Atari game but knew
nothing else really about them as a band
Jayme had heard of Led Zeppelin (couldn't name a song) and
had never heard of Pearl Jam, I went out with her anyways

our first date was April 16th, 1994
Jayme's junior prom
it was a little over a week after Kurt had checked out
Pearl Jam was performing on Saturday Night Live
that night, 3 songs, two from their new album *Vitalogy*
it was a really big night for grunge rock

when I told Jayme I skipped it to be at her prom
I didn't feel like she was as impressed
as my sacrifice should have warranted
of course my brother promised me he'd tape it
I had my friend Geoff record it also just to be safe

prom was a classic 90's prom
I had a ridiculous rented tux fashioned after the one
Val Kilmer wore in *Tombstone*
my favorite movie at the time
Chasing Amy was still years away

Jayme had her hair curled and piled on her head
to distract from her braces
I wore my clear retainer rather than my wire one
Jayme's shoes were dyed to match her dress
I gave her a wrist carnation to avoid the awkward pinning
she gave me boutonniere and stabbed me twice putting it on

to confirm that it was a big night we had dinner at
Red Lobster before the dance
I even sprung for the shrimp pizza appetizer

then something happened at dinner
this girl from this other school that just happened to ask
me to her prom at a speech tournament made me laugh
she was genuinely funny and smart
she had horrible taste in music, but other than that
she was cool

at the dance, we swayed to Color Me Badd's
I Adore Mi Amore
we fought for our right to party with the Beastie Boys
she put her head on my should during Journey's *Open Arms*
(which actually was a good song even though they weren't
from Seattle)
and then as is the case with 70% of all proms the final dance
was *Stairway to Heaven*

I fell in love in a high school gym in 1994
while Jimmy Page set the mood

Jayme and I still dance to *Stairway* from time to time
it's a great song, but it's a hard song to slow dance to

it's really easy at the start
everything is melodic
as the two of you move along though
the tempo picks up and you either have got to be really in
time with your dancing partner
or you both have to release and do your own
individual dance thing for awhile

the payoff though is if you can find each other again
after the fast, rougher part
you can hold each other for the magical
melodic end of the song where time nearly stops

as Plant sings the last line slowly
your eyes can meet
and you can know that as
you wind on down the road
you've found everything
you're looking for

Evenflow

It's 1991
Fall
I'm in my basement
Listening for the first time to this
Unknown band out of Seattle
They're named Pearl Jam
Track 2, *even flow,* comes on...
Everything changes for me
In a basement
In the fall of 1991

It's 1995
Spring
I'm at a planetarium
With Jayme, *even flow* is blasting as
Lasers beam images on the ceiling
We're wearing 3-D glasses
I hear a fool screaming with joy
Jayme tells me I'm a spaz
I breath in the fog machine smoke deep
And tell her I love her

It's 1992
Winter
For the first time
I'm watching the video for *even flow*
Pearl Jam is huge now
I watch Eddie Vedder climb up the balcony
And dive fearlessly into the crowd below
I spill my Mountain Dew in awe

It's 1998
Summer
I'm in St. Louis
With Jayme, Whitt and Whitt's girlfriend
We drove all night
It's their first Pearl Jam show
At one point Eddie wears a construction hat
Jayme says he's funny
Whitt almost kicks a guy's ass for pushing his girl
I scream myself hoarse

It's 1994
Spring
Pearl Jam is playing on SNL
They get three songs instead of two because they're the
Biggest band in the world now
I'm not at home watching
I'm at a prom and not even mine
I met a girl at a speech tournament
She asked me to prom
Her name is Jayme
She likes Madonna and Arlo Gutherie
I can't see how it's going to work
I pray my brother remembers to tape SNL
Maybe they'll play *even flow*...

Is this girl trying to kiss me?!

Everything changes for me
At a prom
In 1994

It's 2000
Fall
Lubbock, Texas
Jayme and I have moved here
Pearl Jam is in front of us
Singing a Buddy Holly song
Jayme and I scream from the front row
In an hour Eddie will pull Jayme up on stage
Her Courtney Cox to his Bruce Springsteen
Jayme will take bows with the band and get her picture with
Ed
I will scream myself hoarse
Telling Jayme and Pearl Jam I love them

It's 1995
Summer
Red Rocks
With Dave, I've never seen Pearl Jam before
Did Eddie just ride out on stage on a bicycle?

It's 2003
Summer
Road trip to Oklahoma City
I write "Pearl Jam Forever" on the side of my car in Spirit
Foam not realizing that it's made specifically for windows
It stains the paint, our car says "Pearl Jam Forever" forever
Jayme sighs

It's 1999
Summer
My wedding
Jayme doesn't let me play *even flow*
As we run out of the church

It's 1998
Summer
Fiddler's Green, Denver
With Aaron, a girl has just implied
She'll *do anything* for our front row tickets
I turn her down instantly, Aaron sighs

It's 2006, I'm in Mountainview with Jayme
It's 2000, I'm in Albuquerque with Holder
It's 2009, I'm in San Diego with a couple from Florida
I met on the Pearl Jam message boards
It's 2003, I'm in San Antonio with Jayme
It's 2003, I'm in Council Bluffs with Dustin
It's 2008, I'm in Santa Cruz with Holder
It's 2004, I'm in Toledo with Pat
It's 2006, I'm in Los Angeles with Doug
It's 2008, I'm in Santa Barbara, I meet Eddie Vedder

It's 2007
Summer
3 a.m., I'm home with Carter
Warming up his bottle
He stares at me in my arm
My wrist acts as Goldilocks, confirms the milk is
Just right
My son drinks the bottle and I notice
The bottle says "even flow"
I smile and quietly put on a Pearl Jam record
Everything has changed for me

It's 2008
Spring
VH1 is doing a classic rock weekend
Carter is taking steps with more confidence
Than his 10 months should allow
The video for *even flow* comes on
Carter watches the colors and bobs to the beat
Eddie climbs the balcony again, as he has for the last
One hundred times I've watched this video

Carter giggles
Jayme smiles
Eddie leaps

I feel Mr. Vedder's mid-air stillness
His peace

This is our life here in these final days of rock and roll

Jayme
Carter
Me

We take Eddie's lead

We all dive in

Encore

November and Everything After...

November of 1989 was about two very different girls
both of whom were firsts
my sister Tessie and a girl named J___

my sister was born early November, two days before my 13th
birthday
her arrival was a big deal as she was the first girl after three
boys
my parents weren't the ultrasound type so it was a surprise
I got called out of 5th period Biology (which I hated
so score one already for new sister Tessie) as my aunt was
waiting to drive me to the hospital
I was dying inside
that night this girl J___ in my class was hosting
the first boy-girl party ever
this girl J___, whom I liked, whom I thought maybe even
liked me a little
wanted me to come to her party
a party with girls
and not wrinkly, newborn girls that I was related to, but
hot girls from school that me and my fellow seventh grade
compatriots could potentially make out with!
I was horrified my parents would make me stay at the
hospital and
I would die
alone
a virgin
unkissed
and
unloved

at the hospital I tried to be interested in the small
nine-pound bundle
staring out at me from a blanket wrapped so tightly around
her that I doubted whether she was getting any circulation
but I was already thinking about what I was going to wear to
the party
was I going to be late?
would they let me leave soon?
would I get to kiss J___ or not?
should I bring my new Bon Jovi cassette?
were the rumors about spin the bottle true?
this was a party where there would be girls and boys
and this was totally unprecedented, nothing had prepared
me for this!

my dad understanding the magnitude of the upcoming fête
having himself been a thirteen-year-old boy
at some point in his life
finally drove me home after making me take
the obligatory Polaroid with Tessie
I got to the party twenty minutes late
not realizing that this was cool
the Polaroid was a big hit, all of the girls wanted to see it
I thought I was scoring
not realizing that girls thinking you're "so cute" and "sweet"
isn't really a good thing in junior high (or ever really)
if making out with them is your ultimate goal

the party, by 1989 standards, was epic
we drank Mountain Dew
we ate Cool Ranch Doritos
we listened to good music (Ratt, Roxette)
we listened to terrible music (MC Hammer, The Simpsons)
everyone kind of bounced around
sort of like we were dancing
but not really
we all ended up spinning a bottle in a garage, giggling
all of it culminating with me and J__
standing beside her house
in the dark
while Bon Jovi's *I'll Be There 4 U*
played on a boom box from inside the garage
it was, by 1989 standards, romantic

I remember my heart trying to crawl out of my mouth
and run down the street, my hands firmly placed in my
stone washed jeans so J____ wouldn't notice them shaking
we couldn't really figure out how you initiate kissing so
we counted aloud
one
two
three
and then pressed our lips together, softly and briefly
like we were a couple of actors in a movie from the 1930's

look, I'd love to tell you that it was a passionate kiss
or that it led to a relationship
but this kiss was five years before I actually fell in love
this kiss was five years before my first kiss with Jayme
which was *that* passionate kiss that led to a
relationship, marriage, kids...

this kiss with J___ in 1989
it wasn't *that* kiss
but it was my first and
it was sweet and
it was innocent

like the kid in the picture
smiling
holding his new baby sister
bright eyes looking out upon
November and everything after

About the Author

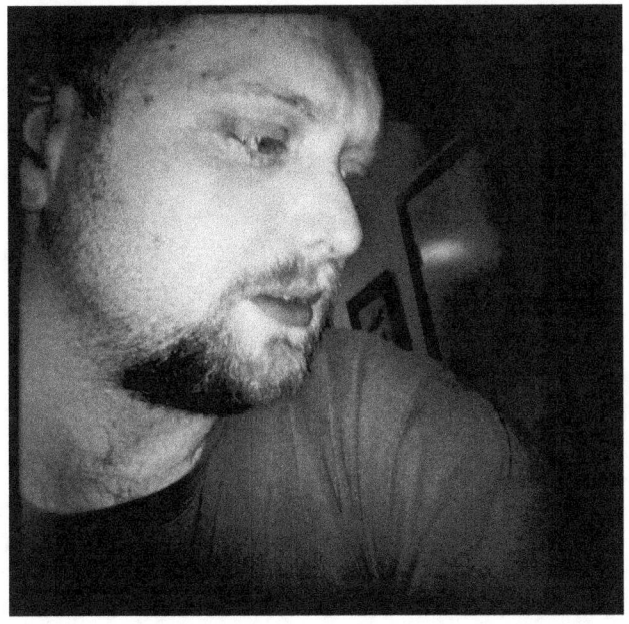

Damien Stednitz has written three previous collections of poetry and short fiction: <u>On The Rise I Guess</u>, <u>We Are Our Own Lions</u>, and <u>The Carter Variations</u>. <u>We Are Our Own Lions</u> was recently reissued in 2011 and is available online.

Stednitz's work has also appeared in various online and print magazines and journals including *Speechless Magazine* and *Contemporary Rhyme*. Stednitz has been a featured reader at various poetry events around California and was poet laureate of Sunland, CA 2008-2010. He lives in Los Angeles with his wife and their two children.

Book Two:

Paper-Thin Wings
and Stupid Love

by
Tessie Stednitz

An Egoboy Studios Production

November and Everything After:
Paper-Thin Wings and Stupid Love

Copyright © 2011 by   Tessie Stednitz
Published by   Egoboy Studios
                        Sunland, CA

This book is a work of fiction. Names, characters, places and incidents are products of the author's imagination or are used fictitiously. Any resemblance to actual events or locales or persons, living or dead is entirely coincidental.

All photos © 2011 by Kenneth "Ty" Kelley.

First Printing   May, 2011

This one is for Sarah, who never ceases to make me feel infinite.

Love you, Little Sister.

Author's Note:

I need to start off by thanking my brother, Damien. This has been a crazy journey and I've learned so much. You got me started writing this crazy poetry stuff and I'm so glad that we could team up and make something magical.

Ty Kelley also deserves thanks and recognition for handling all of my photos. You are one badass photographer.

I'd also like to thank my family and friends, especially those who pledged on our Kickstarter page. You are literally the reason this book is being published.

The following individuals deserve special recognition for support that was above and beyond:

Emily Smythe
Seth Stednitz and Melissa Fowler
Connor Stednitz
Luke Hoffman
Matthew Vicars
Sally Stednitz
Patrick Sather
Shelia Hansen
Jim McKain
Ryan Syrek
Aaron Blackman

Table of Contents

Paper-Thin Wings

Stupid Love

Paper-Thin Wings and Stupid Love

Paper-Thin Wings

For the Tin Man

I have started this poem one hundred times.

This poem about how heartless you are.

How you so remarkably resemble the Tin Man that you
speak of so often.

I had
metaphors and similes,
rhymes and rhythms,
limericks and lines

pouring from my fingertips
that would have rusted you over
until you were broken
into
dull,
tin
pieces.

Then I saw it
briefly,
for a few moments,
a flash of heart.

A heart, buried in the depths of your chest
protected by tin and pride, but still there
beating,
pulsing.

I cannot reach it.

I cannot touch it.

I no longer yearn for it.

I am not the one meant to forever
unearth the wonders
of your hidden heart.

But one day,
maybe a not too terribly distant day,
the girl who is meant to
will find your heart.

Maybe she will love you Tin Man.

I cannot.

Don't give up hope Tin Man.

Never give up hope.

My Epic Verbal Cluster-Fuck

I don't know if this is technically a poem.
I see it more as an
epic, verbal cluster-fuck of
angerhatefearconfusionsadnesspain.

Because here's the deal:
you hurt me.

You did.

I'm sure you're aware of this from the many weeping sprees
I've had in front of
pretty much everyone we know.

You did not break my heart,
but there's a
fracture right down the middle.
But, I'm healing.

I am angry with you.
From your behavior last night I guess
you're angry with me too.
I think maybe we need the time to be angry
because things didn't work out the way
either of us hoped they would.

I care about you so much.
I do.
I know we're going get through this,
whatever "this" is.

When you said you wanted to know me forever
I know you meant it.
I feel the same way.

I want us to get back to the point where we're excited to see
each other.
I used to get a huge hug from you because we were happy
that the weekend was here and we could hang out.

We just got to be friends.

Right now we avoid each other's eyes and let drinks make the
other disappear.
I want my friend back.
I want my friend back so bad it hurts.
I don't really like this kid who ignores me and makes me cry.

I don't know if this is technically a poem.

I see it more as an
epic, verbal cluster-fuck of
hopehappinessfriendshipfaith.

So I hope you read this and don't get angry.
I hope you understand where I'm at.
Maybe we can get to that great place we used to be:
friends.

My Beautiful Figurative Heart

See this?
What I am holding out to you
right now?

This is my heart.
Well, not my literal heart because that would be
disgusting and I would be dead.

But this,
this is my heart.
This is my beautiful, figurative heart.
I am holding it out to you.

You know he wanted it, but he couldn't have it
because it didn't fit into his palms.
It was too big.
It was meant for your hands only.

And yet we're dancing around this like two seventh graders
at a school dance who have to stand six inches apart to
leave room for Jesus.

Jesus I want to be so close to you that I can feel your heart
beating and feel your breath rise and fall.
I feel like we're walking the tight rope of

a
r
e

w
e
?

a
r
e
n
'
t

w
e
?

You know if something doesn't happen soon one of us is
going to fall off.

Look,
this is my heart.

This is my beautiful,
figurative heart.

Take it.

Please.

Pandora

I dream about you.

I dream about you every single night.

This would be understandable if I saw you all the time,
but I don't, not anymore.

I don't see you,
talk to you,
think about you
until I sleep.

Until I close my eyes and give way to my subconscious.
I've taken to watching horror movies before bed hoping to
escape from you into nightmares and yet there you are.
You are just the same.

But when I wake up, it's not to your face.
I wake up to his.
You know, the guy I originally left so I could be with you.
Him and I got back together after whatever we were ended.

If he ever read this poem I would be so fucked.
Your name is Pandora to us.
If it is ever mentioned
every horrible disease and plague will writhe and wriggle its
way into my relationship with him.
It would be ruined, nothing left but ashes and embers.

I dream about you.

I dream about you every single night.

I am waiting in terror for the morning I say your name
instead of his.

My Stomach and Heart Hurt

There's a little boy at the daycare where I work
who could have been our kid.

I don't mean that in the creepy let's-kidnap-him-and-raise-
him-as-our-own kind of way.

I mean that in the he-kind-of-looks-like-our-facial-features-
combined kind of way.

He's a sweet kid.
He's smart, like you.
He's impulsive, like me.
He sometimes calls me "Mom".

It used to make me smile,
but now it just makes
my stomach and heart hurt
because we aren't together anymore.

We are done.

This little boy is still there.

Reminding me of the fact that you and I got to that point,
that point where we talked about:
kids,
marriage,
the whole shebang.

This little boy is still there.

We are done.

Our little boy is still there,
reminding me that we never got that far.

To Her, On Her Wedding Day

How appropriate,
a white dress.

No one seems to see the irony in that
except me.

Your hair is perfectly pulled into a proper princess 'do.
A white wedding,
something he more than likely paid for.

Like everything else in your life.

Spoiled,
even at twenty three,
always nabbing what
you want.

I know the saying goes,
"Something borrowed,
something blue."

I never thought the something borrowed
would be the love of my life
and the something blue

would
be
me.

The Crumbling of My Foundations

My diary is bleeding ink from the pages that held your name.
Each letter drips out like the tears slipping from the bottom
of my face.
They drop on to the floor and disappear
like magic
with no one but me to remember that they were once there.

My back is forgetting the feel of your fingertips
just like the muscles of my hands are forgetting your touch.
Soon they will become wrinkled and feeble
with not even the strength of a child's grasp.

My back will no longer arch with the sensation of your
fingers gliding along it.
It will gradually bend forward until I become haggard
like the crooked creature in a story I once read.

My eyes are forgetting your appearance.
The retinas are detaching from your rough lips.
Soon the sapphire sea you saw in them will no longer meet
with the emerald city I saw in yours.
The sea will be swallowed by the harsh, white tundra.

My mind is forgetting you.
Like a snake slinking through my memories and devouring
each second that included you.
Soon it will crawl into my vocal chords and I will not even
remember your name.

You will flicker out.

You will become nothing
to me.

My Heart is a Fool

It's funny how my heart never forgot
childhood love.

The summer nights filled with
fireflies,
flashlight tag,
and fireworks.

When the boy I fell in love with
before I knew what love meant
left the land of cornfields and plains
for the land of oceans and beaches

my heart didn't let go.

It buried my love.
My heart allowed this love to remain dormant
until that boy returned.

But my heart is a
wandering fool
and when I had the chance to
unearth that infinite love,
to let that love soar on paper-thin wings

I made the wrong choice.

Before I could turn around
and make amends
he was gone.

His heart was given to another.

So now my heart
must bury that love once more.

Make it dormant
until it beats no more.

Pall Mall Blues

We were like cigarettes.

We knew lighting up would be hazardous to our health...
we did it anyway.

We inhaled,
took that first breath of each other,
reeling in the lightheaded euphoria.

We glowed,
creating a heat meant only for us.

We burned,
sending smoke into the atmosphere
like two ghosts who have found redemption.

Then we were reduced to ashes.

We became a glowing ember that faded out over time.

Love,
like cigarettes,
never lasts as long as you want it to.

For Wendy

You had a name:
Wendy.

A name bound for adventure.

I gave you this room,
decorated with mermaids, Indians, fairies,
and a boy flying across your ceiling.

"Second star to the right and straight on 'til morning!"

That is what he would have said to you,
my Wendy.

But you
cannot fly,
cannot grow.
Now I will not
hear your laughter.

I will not hear you
because an enemy
worse than crocodiles,
worse than pirates,
worse than Hook,
has broken me.

My body has broken like a pirate breaks a lost boy.

Now all I hear is
tick,
tick,
tick.

The Vitality of Romance

You said romance is
dead.

You told me there are no epic loves
worthy of
poetry or history.

But I see romance in all its
splendor and vitality.

Romance is on the 101.

It takes the form of a man
running desperately along the shoulder
of the busiest freeway in Los Angeles.

He is sweating in his finest suit and clutching a
bouquet of white roses.
He wipes his brow and checks his watch.
Maybe he is praying to every God he can remember that
he's not too late.

Maybe he's praying that he will get there in time
to stop her,
to tell her,
to love her.

You're wrong.

Romance is not dead.

It's on the 101.

The Last Time I Try To Tell You How I Feel About You

The only way I can honestly tell you
how I feel about you
is through poetry
or substantial amounts of booze.

Poetry seems slightly more romantic and
less likely to induce nausea
so here I am.

I should have ended up with you.

I feel it in my gut,
my heart,
and every other major organ.

I feel like this is a sign.

I know we had a chance to be together.
Be together in a way that I used to dream about
when I was six years old:

epic together,
me and you together,
us together.

We had that chance
and I screwed it up because I had
a moment of doubt.

Now you're with someone else
and every time you say her name
my heart cracks a little.

These daily, tiny fractures that are
weakening the whole.
So, this has to be the last time.

This has to be the last time
I try and tell you how I feel about you:

I want to be with you.

I want
epic together,
you and me together,
us together.

Stupid
Love

Britney

I am about to be attacked by Britney Spears...

her weapon is the album after the breast implants but before the crazy

my car is halted at a stop light and she sneaks up on me
like a blonde, southern, pop-star ninja
the beat reaches out of my radio and finds its way into my ears

I resist

the croaky-singy thing she does makes me want to slap her
the constant pleas of "baby" make me want to kill myself
but as she sings on, my fingers start tapping the wheel

Britney's beat is beating away at my defenses
my hips began to swivel like Shakira herself

I cannot leave Britney alone!

I belt out the words, my body shakes to the beat
against the seat belts barely contained!

I have become toxic, I am slipping under!

I hear laughing next to me and I realize my windows are down...

well hey hipster in the car next to me listening to some
obscure band I've probably never heard of
I refuse to apologize to you!

why?

it's Britney, bitch

Facebook (Likes to Bitch Slap Me)

I hate it when Facebook bitch slaps me.

1 New Notification:

A really hot girl also commented on your boyfriend's status.

A really hot, exotic-looking girl also commented on your boyfriend's status.

A really hot, exotic-looking girl whose profile picture is her in only panties and a vest also commented on your boyfriend's status.

A really hot, exotic-looking girl whose profile picture is her in only panties and a vest because she's a model also commented on your boyfriend's status.

A really hot, exotic-looking girl whose profile picture is her in only panties and a vest because she's a model from Europe also commented on your boyfriend's status.

How the fuck am I supposed to compete with that!?

I am a curvy, blue-eyed, blonde-haired girl from America!

That's as exotic as apple fucking pie!

Thanks, Zuckerburg. Thanks.

Hey, Little Girl

Little Girl,
you are fourteen.

Stop taking off your clothes
and sending naked pictures to boys.
These boys see nothing but
flat chests and inexperienced lips.

Little Girl,
being orange and acting like you're from
Jersey Shore
does not make you hot,
it makes you a moron.

Little Girl,
don't be a tramp,
be a lady.

Pick up your
dolls,
play with your
toy ponies.

Enjoy your childhood while you
still have it.

Don't let MTV
spread your legs.

Because I Am Female

you are the girl that makes me insecure
which is no good for you because since I am female
I am going to lunge at you like a
fucking King (or should I say Queen) Cobra

you will fall before you even feel my
fucking venom
my poison is in words, girl

I will say your ass is fat!
and so are your thighs!
and so are your hips!
and so is your stomach!
and so are your arms!
and so is your face!

I will attack every flaw that you may have not wanted to
expose
and because I am female, sugar, I will find it

I am like a
fucking archeologist
I am Miss Indiana Fucking Jones
I will find every
clogged pore
non-plucked eyebrow
unshaven leg
and I will bring those out for the world to see

my fangs will destroy you
you are the girl who makes me insecure
my cobra strike will end you
you, the girl who makes me insecure

I am the girl that is insecure
which is no good for me, girl, because since I am female
I know none of the venom I want to spit about you is true

you are
absolutely gorgeous
and nice
even sweet
your nectar is in your words, girl
kind eyes and words

you are a friendly, nice mongoose to my cobra

I am none of the things you are
I am the girl that is insecure
that may be why the man I love left me for you

Ode to Hot Neighbor

Oh, Hot Neighbor,
how I adore your hotness!

You are the reason I look forward to spring
during the cold, bleak, and dark months of winter.

For when the sun emerges and the flowers bloom,
your shirt disappears!

I get to ogle
your sexy, six-pack and
your perfectly mohawked hair
as you mow our front yard.

Hot Neighbor,
I know your name is Jake.

"Jake" doesn't adequately describe your hotness.

So I will continue to call you "Hot Neighbor"
until my lease is up.

College Hippies

Each day, as I walk back to my dorm from class
I spot many a barefoot hippie trotting along campus.
Hippies with a smug look of satisfaction drawn along their
faces.

It's as if by going barefoot to class, they are somehow proving
something.
Showing all of us how cool and non-conforming they are by
refusing footwear.

"Look, I don't even wear shoes! That's how much of an
individual I am!"

I watch one particularly hip hippie step in a large luggie
puddle made by a bulky jock.
I wonder how cool hippie boy feels now that he is walking
with chewing tobacco stained mucus on his foot.

Keep fighting The Man, hippie with your nasty foot.
Keep fighting The Man.

Joe vs. Steve

How dare Joe!

How dare he try to be better than Steve.

Steve, you know Steve,
constantly in his
green striped shirt,
singing with *his* dog
Blue.

I used to wake up early
just to sing *The Mail Song* with Steve.

Steve always nailed the last note of the song
with raspy belting and jazz handing.

Joe can't hit that note.

Just because Steve "went to college"
Joe gets to jump the shark and suck out any
coolness that *Blue's Clues* had left.

Joe,
that gap-toothed,
push-over.

I bet Blue secretly hates him.

I do.

Joe is a tool.

Bro

I met a new boy.

He was "Bro-tastic"
in that he wore multiple polos
with the collars all popped,
a hat tilted to the side
and had both ears pierced with diamond studs.

Thirty seconds after our introduction,
he attempted to get in my pants.

"I just got out of a bad relationship
and could really use some...
rejuvenation."

What the hell?

In what sick, warped dimension does that shit
actually work?

Maybe he does need some rejuvenation.
I could rejuvenate my knee
right into his balls.

Twilight

I have no idea what the hell is going on.

All around me girls are panting and moaning
as if they are about to climax.

This is the worst movie I have ever seen.

Ever.

Yet girls are falling all over themselves for a guy
who is not that hot and definitely not that talented.

As I emerge from the theater I exclaim,

"I want my money back. That was freakin' awful!"

As soon as these words escape my mouth
I hear gasps all around me.

I am swarmed by hundreds of hormonal, hate-filled eyes
trying to stake me with glares.

If Buffy was here she totally would go slayer on their asses
for me.

Sarah (a.k.a. Skipper)

I used to have a life-sized Barbie car.

Well, life-sized for an eight-year-old.

I would drive that baby up and down
the block of my childhood home.

My platinum-blonde hair blowing in the breeze.

I was perfectly Barbie-like.

Then the sun went down
and the battery died.

So I made my little sister, Sarah, push me
around the block.

Come on,
would Barbie push herself?

Hell no,
she'd make Skipper
do that shit.

Paper-Thin
Wings and
Stupid Love

November and Everything After

November of 2002 was about two very different boys,
both of whom were firsts,
a baby named Mickael and a boy named R.J.

Mickael was born in early November
the day before my 13th birthday.

My mother, who ran her own daycare from home,
broke her long standing rule that she would not watch any
boys when a close family friend gave birth to Mickael.

A boy who from the moment he was born you knew would be
a freckled ginger.

The news of Mickael's birth was overshadowed
by a rumor rolling through the hallways of my middle school.

Supposedly, R.J, a tan, blonde, future football star,
a twelve-year-old who was already rocking six-pack abs,
the hottest boy in the seventh grade,
wanted to make out with me.

Me.

When Mickael was brought to our home for the
family to "ooo" and "aah" over
the only thing on my mind was how
R.J. was waiting at the movie theater.

This was the place middle school kids go to
make out. All the privacy you need in the back row.

I held Mickael.
It was my first time holding a newborn.
He was so fragile.

I was nervous that I would somehow hurt him.

I adhered to the rules of supporting necks
and not squeezing too hard
so Mickael remained in one piece.

His eyes were shining and constantly searching my face.

Everything he saw was a new discovery.

He squirmed and slobbered,
and I was terrified he might drool
all over the outfit I had taken almost
two days to put together
for my romantic rendezvous with R.J.

My father saw my restlessness,
understanding the nerves and excitement
that build around a first date.

We snapped a digital photo of
me holding the bundled Mickael
and then jetted off to the theater.

As my dad dropped me off in front of the theater,
he kissed my cheek,
handed me ten dollars, and told me to have fun.

There was a look in his eyes,
like he knew that after tonight
I would be different.

R. J. and I sat in the top row as expected.
Neither one of us willing to raise the armrest that
separated us and prevented the initial
arm-around-the-shoulder prelude.

R.J. eventually plucked up the courage, raised the armrest
and placed his arm around my trembling shoulder.

We were watching *Pirates of the Caribbean*.

Well, pretending to watch it because my
heart was rocketing itself against my chest
and I couldn't pay attention because
I could only think about R.J.'s arm
and I was worrying about if his braces
would prevent us from really being able to kiss.
Do couples really get their braces locked to each other?
Do you go to the ER or the dentist?

Then R.J. turned his head as
I turned mine
and our lips met.

Jonny Depp muttered, "If you were looking for an optimal
moment, mate that was it."

I wish I could tell you that it was
a passionate, perfect kiss.

It wasn't.

It was sloppy and silly
and R.J. and I didn't
blossom into love and romance.

In fact, we didn't talk much after that.

But a boy I did become close to
and grow to love was Mickael.

The mischievous, wonderful little brother I never had.
That kiss with R.J. in 2002

it wasn't *that kiss,*
but it was my first,
a new discovery.

It was awkward,
like the girl in that picture.

It was innocent,
like the baby in that picture.

That picture of me holding Mickael,
smiling.

A new baby that would be like a little brother to me.

Bright eyes looking out upon
November and everything after.

About the Author

Tessie Stednitz's work has previously been published by
Poetry Superhighway. In 2011 Tessie won the American
Forensics Association collegiate national championship for
Program Oral Interpretation. Stednitz also qualified to
compete in the 2011 National Poetry Slam Competition in
Boston. <u>Paper-Thin Wings and Stupid Love</u> is her debut
collection of poetry. Stednitz lives in Omaha.